OMBRA-E-SPECCHIO (SHADOW & MIRROR)

"BE THE LIGHT AND MIRROR IN THE WORLD FULL OF SHADOWS"

AYSHA SWALIHA

Contents

Contents

Contents

Contents

Contents

Dedicated

To my loving parents

AND

my beloved grandparents

Author's Note

Aysha Swaliha :" Now when you are reading this book, while flipping the pages. I'm flying around like a firefly with a hope of change within us"

My heartfelt gratitude to all of you beautiful souls ,who chose this book to read.In the world full of shadows i was searching for the light. I truly hope my words reach depth of your hearts and mind & bring positive change in your life.

In this life we face many challenges & blessings, which makes us beautiful and differentfrom each other, that's when we find who we really are. All these 21 years of my life taughtme many things, from letting tears flow to holding it back and then believing in the fact of turning tears into light of hope.I encourage you to do the same or even better.

So here i prefer to be among the people who voiced their thoughts breaking every barrier,who chose to be the light & mirror by taking up the courage to write down it in words ....

Instagram@aysha_swaliha_

Acknowledgements

"As there is morning after night, rain after summer heat. Every story has to start somewhere. Likewise my journey had to start somewhere, These roads aren't always beautiful and easy as it looks to others. Every small success has a story of struggle & hard work and the most important support and love froM the loved ones.

First of all i thank Almighty God for blessing me with this gift, and guiding me all the way .

I started to write when i was 13 years ,it was back in my highschool days when i realised the hidden treasure i had. I thank all those friends of mine who knowingly or unkonowingly made me realise it.

And a special thanks to a teacher suvarna ma,'am who believed in me and encouraged me to write more.

I was in 10th when i stopped writing , i lost interest in writing. if mom haven't kept aking me back then the reason of me quittng. i think i would have been permanently lost as a poet or a writer. Thank you is just too small word to express how thankful i am to Mom & Dad, you both are amazing.....

And a big thanks to my brothers Umar and Abubakar for always supporting me and finding mistakes and guiding me through without you both self publishing would have been lot more tiresome.

THANKyou my classmates your exitement of seeing me as a published author and seeing my solo book gave me a lot of strenght.

and also my lectures thank you soo much for encouraging me when you got to know i write poems and quotes. all of you are loving people the world need.

its my pleasure that i met Nourin N.K through instagram, poet of book untying my wings , who became a close friend eventually.without her help, guidence , encouragement...i would have not been this confident in publishing my own book.

thanks to my special and dearest friends who always encouraged me in this journey words aren't enough to describe . There are two dearest people who also helped me along with my brothers while i was publishing this book, Nidha thank you for your patience with me when i kept changing the designs and kept making you choose one between the other . thank you (to the one who didn't wanted to be metioned)you beautiful soul ....

thank you my instagram friends for your love when i write something.

From bttom of my Heart Thank you everyone ...... the one i mentioned and one i didn't you all are the beautifulest souls i know..........

1. Glow UP

Hey, you
Yes you dear,
It's time to get up
& let the sorrows go
It's time to blow up your ideas
You should first be proud of yourself
No-one will be
Proud of you
Until you succeed
Don't get be motivated
by people's comment
Because
Today they say one thing
Tomorrow another
So stay focused
Don't get distracted by
These things
It's you who should glow up

2. Value

Every minute of your life
Is a test
Whether to win or to loose
It depends upon you

3. Mistakes

When you make a mistake,
You learn a lesson
Now you learnt a lesson
So don't repeat it

4. Peace

PEACE,
to see it's just five lettered word
But in real
It's the most precious & valuable
PEACE is the climate of freedom

5. Fear

Fear of loosing something
Is a terrible feeling
Isn't it?

6. It's all about.....

Life is all about

Task & challenges

So live it , complete it

&

Peace is yours

7. Worry

Worrying about things
that doesn't even exist
Is a terrible feeling

8. Bother

Why bother about future,
Work hard & smart
And leave everything upon god

9. Smart

Everyone works hard,
What really matter is
Whether you work smart
Or not

10. I dream of my dreams

I dream of my dreams,
Dreams which make me happy,
Dreams that keeps me awake.
I dream of my dreams,
Every night and every day
And it keeps me awake
From every Strom and the war.
When I was breaking down,
It kept me brave and strong
And I don't wanna let it goo,
And now I'm living my dream,
By dreaming of my dreams.
I dream of my dreams,
Dreams Which makes me happy,
Dreams that kept me alive,
When I was shattered into pieces ,
and my heart was breaking down,
Breaking down n down,
And Now I'm living my dream,
By dreaming of my dream..

11. Wiser more

Stay down to earth
& calm down
be wise and
be truthfu

12. Dreams

Sometimes even dream
can disturb you
I'm not talking about that dream
rather
It's about dream when
We are asleep

13. Good

When you start to do good,
many things will come in your way
to stop you,
Yet, it's up to you to decide
Whether to give up
Or stay up

14. Ant

Whenever you think of quitting
Your dream goal,
Just think of the Ant
which tries to climb,
You will get motivated

15. Warriors

A warrior is the one who knows,
How to act
accordingly to the
Present situation
Without lying

16. Being a warrior

Being a warrior
Isn't easy,
It's a task
Taken by Brave, pious
& trustworthy

17. Power of pen

A pen can be more harmful
then the nuclear bomb
& most helpful like water,
Only depends upon the person
who is writing using it

18. Challenges

Challenges in your life is the
part of life without which
Your life is like lemonade
Without lemon

19. Struggle of creatures

Everyone struggles to build there home
Whoever it is ,whatever it is,
Humans , birds or animals or insects
whatever it may be
Everyone works hard for themselves,
Their families and society.

20. Options

Having too many options are sometimes
Irritable, because there will be more things
You want to do &
You won't be able to focus on one thing

21. Temporary

'Temporary?' isn't always bad"
She loved the way the things where there for her,
But she never knew it won't last for long,
Every things were lovely .
Cool was the way she lived for her dreams,
And everything was so excited.
Amazing was her intrests in so many things,
When she realized everything is temporary, it wasn't too late.
Shocking was when she finally understood that ,
what it means "if you enjoy little moments it makes a big
difference in your life",
Now she felt happy
Even when she's sad she smiled ,
Knowing that it's temporary she gained some patience.

22. Hope

HOPE isn't just a word, those four
lettered word has some
different type of confidence,
will power ,it's special &
It controls our mentality

23. Worth of hope

Life may seem hard for you,
The struggles may be endless,
Tears maybe limitless,
But
Hope isn't worthless.

24. Giving up

My life took several turns,
Ups & downs
And it's still the same,
But
I believe in never giving up

25. Blame

People often blame others
for their own failures,
But deep inside
they blame themselves,
They just don't wanna accept the Truth

26. Feelings...

Year pass, decade pass, people pass,
So does love, everything passes away,
Except for one thing,
Feelings,
This idiot remains the same .

27. Believe

Hundreds of time I fell,
Hundreds of time I got criticised,
Hundreds of time they laughed at me,
Sometimes in front of me &
most of the time behind my back,
But I believe in Almighty God
That billions of time
I'm going to succeed.

28. A note

Listen carefully,
You beautiful soul,
Break all the barriers of hate,
Angerness and revenge.
Build up the connection of love,
Compassion, mercy & kindness.
Leave behind the evil deeds & start the
Noble deeds .

29. Hard

It's easy to give up & Hard to stay up,
Easy to look down & Hard to get up,
Easy to fail but Hard to succeed.
HARD
H-hope high, be
A-ambitious & be
R -ready to
D- dig the treasure

30. Hijab

The day when I wore hijab was the day
When in wore my crown

31. Crown

I'm not in search of job
I'm looking for the crown itself

32. War she fought

From start till the end of war
She was like strong walls of Castle,
Which can stop even the bombs of fire
Because she built herself to a kind of
Personality like ice & fire
Ice that will eat the fire &
fire like Volcano
Which burns
negativity into dust.

33. Meaning?

You call it Destiny, fate, luck,
Whatever you wanna call,
Call it
But the real meaning never change

34. Word

Word has meaning
Until the situation
& the reason
Matches the words

35. If it was easy...

If it was easy
Easy to tell that
I'm not okay
If it was easy
To tell that of all
the things I gone through
Till now,
Why? Is it so hard?
to tell them that I'm not okay
I'm desperately wanna say it all.

36. For good

It's been a while
Since we last talked
Looks like we are parting our ways
For good.

37. Is better to......

When you can't hold back, even after trying
for 100's of times,
It's better to share
them with wise person
Rather than dying everyday

38. You should

Hope for good things
Regret and ask forgiveness from
Lord for the bad deeds
You have done so far..

39. Isn't it??

These rains and weather
It's weird, isn't it??
It gives you the feeling of coolness
Yet warm.

40. Till now

Till now no one understood
Why sound of thunder,
Rain & sounds of nature
are so peaceful
Even though they are noisy.

41. Chance

God has created beautiful things for us
We can't count them all,
isn't it beautiful
Beautiful to have a chance
to worship
The lord of whole universe

42. Mother "Still she won't hate you"

"Like Coffee in winter,
she's the warmth of your cold life,
She's the fire of your rainy days,
She's airconditioner of your summer like heat days,
She wished you everyday and night
All the best my child,
Whether your a girl or boy,
She told, your my boy,
Boy she doesn't mean by gender,
It was her feeling, that your brave,
She lookedup to you,
every second of her life,
But you told yourself,
I really became young,
And then,
everytime she approached you,
You told, your really irritating me mom,
She thought your going through puberty
so why not let him alone?
But she is mom, she couldn't help it ,

Her care for you pushed towards you,
She couldn't stop asking your well being,
What you did in return?
yelled at her,
Ignored her,
Hurted her feelings for whole year,
Then you wish her Happy mothers day,
So why wish her happy mother's day once a year?
When your gonna forget about her
and her well-being for rest of the days,
It's not your fault at some point,
You just became so bzy building your future ,
That you forgot the roots of you,
When is that you last
gave her a bright smile,
and warm hug,
Still she won't hate you
cz she's the mother,
It's never too late,
Go back to her before it's too late..

43. Do good

When you start to do good
Many things will come
In your way to stop you
Yet
It's up to you to decide
Whether
To give up
Or to stay up.

44. Right person

Words aren't enough
to express how you feel
Feelings can't be explained clearly
All it takes
is the right person
To know everything
at right time.

45. Moon in dark sky

Be the moon
in dark sky
Attract the
Arrogant & wise
Change
arrogant to wise

46. Don't think

Hey beautiful soul
Remember
When there is a hill to climb
Don't think that
Waiting will
Make it smaller.

47. Fate

Every system

In the World can be hacked

But

not your Fate

48. All you need

All you need is just
a pinch of courage
& the positivity.

49. Smile of nature

When nature smiles at you
You become crazy........
Because
it speaks the language of
Peace, equality, love
Dedication, kindness,
Passion &
Of every good thing.

50. Will you??

At times, look at kids
& learn from them
enjoy your own company
I.e at times enjoy alone.
If you see a kid enjoying
Smile, join them,
Try once....
Will you??

51. Ray........

A small ray of Hope
& a little fight
against inner fears
Can change a
lot of things
in life.

52. Wings

To fly higher
Don't weigh your wings
Rather
know the strength of it .

53. Smile

*Smile is the best medicine
for the disease of
Hearts and mind.*

54. Weapon

Kindness is the
best weapon to kill
Negativity

55. Perfect

No one is perfect
So stop searching for perfect
Instead search for
A person with good heart

56. This or that

57. You

Unless you find
Who you really are
You won't understand
anything clearly

58. World & Life

At times some are playing
While others are just looking at them
& hoping that one day
they too will play,
Some are laughing and happy
While others,
Crying and sad
This is the World.
Full of scenes & scenarios.
This is Life.

59. Tears

Sometimes holding back your tears
can be harmful
So let it go
don't stop it

60. Book of love

She wasn't the book
he wanted to read
She was the book he was
destined to read

61. Think before you speak

Before criticising and
talking bad about a person,
Think of you being criticised,
If you are senseful
You will know how to behave

62. You.,

It's your mind that can take you anywhere,
It's your faith in God that can keep you so calm,
It's your Heart that can see good in people,
Hey my Friend,
You are Beautiful soul,
It's not all about you,
YET, It's all about YOU.

63. First lie

The last lie I told was……
That I don't need you, &
I can live without you,
Now it seems like it wasn't the last lie,
Rather it was the last truth,
Unfortunately, it was the first lie

64. Tongue

Think before you, open your mouth,
the tongue that lay inside your mouth
Is sharper than the sword,
Hazardous than nuclear weapons,
& dangerous then acids
Just a single word can
destroy everything.

65. Eye

We can make happy face and lie,
Unfortunately, Eyes end up revealing
our emotions, no need of crying......
Eye is an expert.

66. Fate

I won't be there, when you need me,
I won't be there, when you miss me,
Let's call it Fate........
I hope you never hate me .

67. Truth we seek

Little did I know was that,
truth all of us seek in life
Is nothing but
Living in PEACE

68. Should loved myself again……

Why?
Everyone wants to hear what they wants to hear?
Why it looks like others voice of pain,
regret, helplessness can't be heard?
While hoping they will understand, the
Whole life lost in pain,
Everything lost in vain,
Life became like a rain,
Stayed for a while & never came back again,
Moving with pain,
Hoped that I should have loved myself again.

69. Cage

Stuck in cage?
Cage of fear, stress, loneliness, helplessness
Is there no one to help?
Why?
You only know how to console others,
But not yourself
It's not too late,
Now it's time to love yourself
Just a little bit care for yourself
And remember don't forget others
While you care &Love yourself
Care for others &help them
Overcome from what they are going through
& don't just watch them cry
Console them with the words
Of wisdom.

70. Can't describe you

*Words aren't enough to describe you
love,
I can't even write poem on you,
For me you're the
definition of love
You're that air which
silently helps me breath,
&
A friend that make me smile
Oh no,
Once again,
I failed to describe you.*

71. As if i'm dumb

When I see you
I'm mesmerised
Your words
Melts my heart,
Words never help me
When I try to describe
How I feel?
I can't even explain myself
As if I'm dumb.

72. Beauty of sky

When stars shine
It's night
If they are beautiful& bright
Then it is a village
With full of nature & peace
Because
City & it's pollution
Won't let us see
The beauty of sky.

73. Poet

When poets write
they bleed their thoughts
Keeping themself on others shoes
Goes through the same situation
Crys, laughs & breaks down
And then writes it
When readers read
& feel them
That's when poets worth is proven

74. Poetry

They say it's just a poetry,
You can write another one
But only if they knew
the struggles & emotions
We go through
While writing them
Every poem, every thought
Written by a poet
Is attached to them like
A nerve with heart

75. Connection

My eyes stopped looking for you
Mind stopped thinking of you
Heart stopped skipping
When you are around
But
Something more powerful connection
Always drags me towards you.

76. You are beautiful

You, hey you
Yes the one who is reading this
What are you thinking about
So deeply??
You know what, ????
You are Beautiful

77. You & Me

My life & yours seems to be different
In many ways
But
My dreams & yours
are eventually the same

78. Wake up.....

I kept crying until I found out that
Just crying doesn't solve anything
So wake up dear.

79. Are you ready?......

Are you ready to fight your fears,
It's like fighting with yourself,
Every day and night,
Every second and hour,
Are you ready to fight your fears.
It will choke you down and will burn down your mind,
Your will to do things will melt down,
But don't look back, you beautiful soul,
Keep moving forward and fight your fears.
You will never know ,
what it's like to fight your fears,
Until your on the way
For war with your fears.
Are you ready to fight your fears,
It's like fighting with yourself,
Eventually you will get fedup of this war,
You will feel like to run away, like the coward,
Trust me,
And don't ever look back,
until you fight your fears.
As elders said,
'look deep in the eyes of fears'

You will be scared to death
But don't blink,
I said don't blink,
Did you get me?
you beautiful soul.
Cause the second you blink,
All these war you had will be in vain,
And your fears will posses you forever,
Until you fight back your fears.
Hey you beautiful soul,
You should get up and fight back your fears,
Now tell me,
Are you ready to fight your fear.

80. If you re worth it...,

Every person has the ability
to do the things he want,
But
Only the good hearted and wise person
knows the difference between
What he Wants and Needs.
If you are worthy you will be& have both..

81. Looking back

Looking back at times
I feel and get to know that
How dumb and thoughtles I was

82. Changes

someone told me this once,
' things doesn't change
it remains the same'
The thing that changes is only your
Heart/feeling and the way of thinking.
changes in your life is essential
it's a way to be a better version
of yourself.

83. Under the sky

If you can't fall asleep, try
Sleeping under the open sky
I never tried because
I never got the chance to do so,
Even though I can't
Fall asleep
But
One thing I can assure you that
You will feel peaceful because
I slept under the open sky
Once not to fall asleep,
But to watch stars.

84. Yes, We are humans

Hot summer, cold Winter
Cold & chilled rain
Is all that we want
We can't bear one season
Because we are humans.

85. Disturbed

Sometimes even dream can disturb you
I'm not talking about that dream
Rather it's about dream
When we are asleep.

86. Lock down days

Today
even the cities look beautiful
And Peaceful
Like villages

87. Nature

People often hate noisy or loud sounds
Except sound of rain, thunder,
Birds & natural sounds
Which we get in nature.
I love them.
Do you??

88. Stones

Rain sometimes sound like

A small yet

Not too small stones

But it's attractive.

89. winds

These winds I mean
natural cold winds
can drive you crazy
as they bring you
Happiness along,
It's one among the beautiful gift
God has given us .

90. Beauty of nature

When wind strike the
trees andnPlants
It feel like couples are hugging,
What a beautiful scene

91. Smell of soil

The smell of soil
When it rains
It gives a different type of
Fragrance,
Which you can't
Find in perfumes of any kind.

92. Clouds

Clouds are white
yet greyish White
But
Whenever sunlight gazes
at them it gives different
Colour & vibes.

93. Ohh!!!Nature

When wind waves
Isn't the leaves of tree
Look like
Talking to each other?

94. Same sky

When it rains
Or when it's hot summer
When it snows
Or when it's chilled
I know that
Both of us watching
The same sky
Even though
We never know each other.

95. Amazing!!!!

Did you ever see
The rain water
Falling on water?
It's amazingly beautiful.

96. Thunder strom

I just heard the thunder storms
Which was quite loud
&
It was good by the way.

97. Stress

Weight of stress has
the capacity
to destroy your
Health
Like cancerous cells.

98. 100 times??

The words you say
& the steps you take
are most important.
Think 100 times
before you say
Because
Single mistake can
Destroy you.

99. Faith & Knowledge

100. Rain!!!

The drops of water
we call rain,
The smell of soil
Which makes us go crazy
The music of rain
that soothes us
The emotions
filled water flow
Makes every heart
Skip a bit more
Oh,
The beauty of Rain.

101. Heart

Life is beautiful
When you have
Beautiful heart.

102. Work love

If you love the work you do,
Eventually
You will fell in love with it .

103. let go........

I don't know if
I will be brave
Brave enough to let go
Let go who??
Let go the past
& those memories.
Let go the pain
that I'm holding for so long
The failures that
Keeps bothering me
Am I brave enough
to let go the
Comfort zone,
I live in??

104. New Chapter Begins........

Every day is the new chapter
Of life,
Beginning of a
New story
& results of
Your previous days.
Now it's time to open the
New chapter of your life.